This book is sure to be a valuable resource for kids, as well as the adults who support them. Kailey uses a writing voice that is accessible and engaging while offering helpful information and practical coping skills. I could see myself using this with clients as well as with my own children. A great resource!

- Rachel Zobeck, M.Ed, LPC

Alex [the main character in *Anxious Thoughts*] is such a relatable, helpful guide for kids navigating big emotions! Following his example, I'll be able to help the kids in my ministry work through their anxiety in more productive ways so they feel better. Thank you, Kailey, for sharing so many practical ideas through Alex's experiences!

- Sandra Peoples, Author *Unexpected Blessings: The Joy and Possibilities of Life in a Special Needs Family* and Disability Ministry Consultant for the Southern Baptist of Texas

Anxious Thoughts is an incredible resource for parents, teachers, therapists, social workers—basically anyone who works with children! There are so many practical strategies to help children identify what anxiety feels like in their bodies and know what to do when those feelings rise up. As the mother of multiple children who live with anxiety, I can affirm that so many things laid out in this book have been helpful in my own family. I only wish I had had this book when my children were younger!

- Sarah Granger, Mom of four and Host of The Stoplight Approach Podcast

ANXIOUS THOUGHTS

A STORY GUIDE TO COPING WITH STRESS

KAILEY LENTSCH

ILLUSTRATED BY NABEEL HAYDER

Anxious Thoughts: A Story Guide to Coping with Stress
Copyright © 2022 by Kailey Lentsch
Illustrated by Nabeel Hayder

Published by Lucid Books in Houston, TX
www.LucidBooks.com

ISBN: 978-1-63296-529-5 (hardback)

ISBN: 978-1-63296-528-8 (paperback)

eISBN: 978-1-63296-530-1

Special Sales: Lucid Books titles are available in special quantity discounts. Custom imprinting or excerpting can also be done to fit special needs. Contact Lucid Books at Info@LucidBooks.com

To my children, Owen, Ellie, and Landon,
I love being your Momma.

To my husband, Matt,
thank you for encouraging me to chase after crazy dreams.
I love you.

To the God of hope, who sees our worries, doubts, and fears
and so freely offers joy and peace.
(Romans 15:13)

Hi, my name is Alex!

You and I probably
have a lot in common.

I am eight years old.

I like drawing, music,
baseball, and superheroes.

I go to school and love to play
with my family and friends.

Usually, I feel happy or silly or calm.
But sometimes, I feel sad or stressed or anxious.

Stressed and anxious – those are two fancy
words for two emotions.

HAPPY

SILLY

CALM

SAD

OVEWHELMED

ANXIOUS

STRESS is when you feel like the things going on around you are TOO MUCH! Stress can make you feel uncomfortable, tense, or worried.

ANXIETY is when you worry about things or feel afraid of things that are a normal part of your day. Anxiety can make you feel nervous, worried, or scared.

Stress and anxiety are a part of everyone's life.
Feeling a little stressed can help us be
safe and make good choices;

like when a stranger makes me feel uncomfortable,
so I hold my mom's hand to feel safe.

But sometimes, I feel LOTS of stress.

Feeling very stressed or anxious can
make us feel out of control and scared.

When I feel anxious, my body changes.

My heart beats faster and my tummy feels like
it has a hundred butterflies inside of it.

I might shake and I feel like I can't stay still.

My mind and emotions change too.

I feel worried and scared.

Sometimes I feel angry and want to scream as loud as I can.

Other times, I want to run away or go hide somewhere.

Sometimes I want to cry.

Do you ever feel this way?

There are a lot of things that can make people feel stressed or anxious.

Like. . .

A BIG TEST

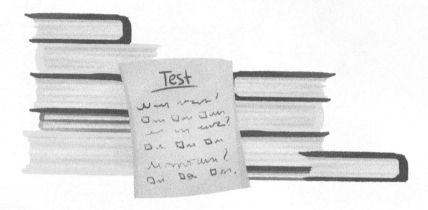

HAVING A LOT OF HOMEWORK

A PERFORMANCE

BEING IN THE DARK

THUNDERSTORMS

SPEAKING IN FRONT OF OTHER PEOPLE

A BIG ⚾ GAME

MEETING SOMEONE NEW

MOVING

GOING SOMEWHERE NEW

THE FIRST DAY OF SCHOOL

There are also a lot of things
that people can do to help them
when they start to feel anxious.

Can I show you some of the things I do?

I can distract myself from what is making me feel anxious.

That means, instead of focusing on what is making me feel stressed or anxious,

I focus on something else.

I can squeeze my ball and think about how squishy it is.

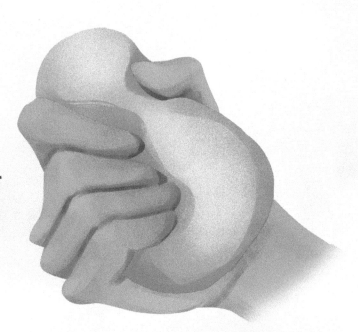

I can play with my fidgets and think about how they pop or spin.

I can play with play-dough,
sand, or water beads
and think about how they
feel in my hands.

I can hug my favorite stuffy and
think about how soft he is.

I can use grounding techniques to bring me back to the moment.

Sometimes I get worried about what will happen in the future, or I get stuck thinking about something that already happened.

Grounding myself reminds me of what is real in the moment I am in.

I can go through my senses.

What are five things I can SEE?

What are four things I can TOUCH?

What are three things I can HEAR?

What are two things I can SMELL?

What is one thing I can TASTE?

I can list things in ABC order.

Alligator. . . bunny. . . cat. . .

dog. . .

elephant. . .

fish. . .

I can pause for a minute.

Sometimes all I need is to walk away from what is making me feel anxious for a moment and then I'm able to reset.

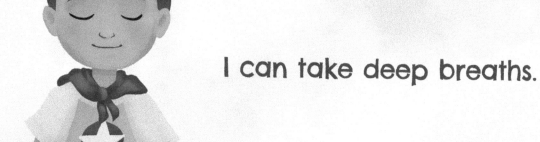

I can take deep breaths.

I can get a drink of water.

I can give myself a hug.

I can think about what makes me happy.

Remembering good, happy things can help me forget what feels bad or scary.

I can make a list of my favorite things.

I can think about what I am thankful for.

I can remember the most fun day.

I can talk, draw, or write about what
is making me feel anxious.

This helps me understand my feelings.

It also helps an adult understand my feelings so
they know how to help me. I can talk to a trusted
adult like my parents, a teacher, or my pastor.

Sometimes just knowing someone is
listening to me makes me feel better.

I can ask for help when something seems too hard to handle by myself.

Adults are pretty good at helping kids.

I can draw a picture that shows what I feel.

I can write in my journal about what I am going through.

Sometimes I only need to do one thing to make me feel better.

Other times, I do a lot of these things!

But one important thing I do whenever I am feeling anxious is to remind myself of what is true.

I AM NOT
my anxiety.

WHAT I FEEL
doesn't make me
WHO I AM.

I CAN BE IN CHARGE
of my thoughts
and feelings.

What can <u>you</u> do when <u>you</u> feel
stressed or anxious?

Kailey Lentsch was born and raised in Ocala, Florida, where she currently lives with her husband, Matt, and their three children. She has a master's degree in social work from the University of Central Florida. Kailey serves her local church by developing children's curriculum and previously worked as a community social worker and special education teacher.

Through her experience working with children in the education system, at church, and with her own children, Kailey recognized a need for age-appropriate instruction on mental wellness. She believes that teaching children about mental wellness and faith sets them up for successful, healthy lives.

CPSIA information can be obtained
at www.ICGtesting.com
Printed in the USA
LVHW070708100822
725536LV00008B/172

9 781632 965295